KINGFISHER

level 3

Record Breakers-
The
Biggest

Claire Llewellyn

KINGFISHER

KINGFISHER

First published 2012 by Kingfisher
an imprint of Macmillan Children's Books
a division of Macmillan Publishers Limited
20 New Wharf Road, London N1 9RR
Basingstoke and Oxford
Associated companies throughout the world
www.panmacmillan.com

Series editor: Heather Morris
Literacy consultant: Hilary Horton

ISBN: 978-0-7534-3057-6
Copyright © Macmillan Publishers Ltd 2012

9 8 7 6 5 4 3 2 1

1TR/1011/WKT/UNTD/105MA

A CIP catalogue record for this book is available from
the British Library.

Printed in China

Picture credits
The Publisher would like to thank the following for permission to reproduce their material. Every care has
been taken to trace copyright holders. However, if there have been unintentional omissions or failure to trace
copyright holders, we apologize and will, if informed, endeavour to make corrections in any future edition.
Top = t; Bottom = b; Centre = c; Left = l; Right = r
Cover Shutterstock/Richard Semik; Pages 4 Getty/Greg Wood/AFP; 5t Getty/Karim Sahib/AFP;
5b Shutterstock/Momentum; 6 Nature Picture Library/Bruce Davidson; 7t Getty/Graeme Robertson;
7b Shutterstock/James Laurie; 8c Frank Lane Picture Agency (FLPA)/Frans Lanting; 8b Shutterstock/Jiri
Hera; 9 Ardea/Jean-Paul Ferrero; 12 Science Photo Library (SPL)/Louisa Preston; 13 FLPA/Frans Lanting;
16 Getty/AFP; 17 Shutterstock/Richard Semik; 18 Corbis/Joe Skipper/Reuters; 19 Corbis/Boris Roessler/epa;
21 SPL/TVT; 22 Ardea/Adrian Warren; 23 Getty/Pemba Dorje Sherpa/AFP; 24 Shutterstock/Galyna Andrushko;
25 Shutterstock/Armin Rose; 26,27 & 28-29 SPL/NASA; all other images Kingfisher artbank

Contents

Big, bigger, biggest

How big are you? Over one metre tall? That's quite big, but it's not as big as some of the things in this book! They are so big that they have broken all the records. They are the biggest things of their kind. The saltwater crocodile is the biggest **reptile** in the world. Read about it on page 9.

Think big!
What is BIG? Well, that depends on your own size. How big would a blackbird seem if you were a grub?

This is the tallest skyscraper in the world. Where is it? Find out on page 14.

Do you know which mountain is the highest in the world? Check out the facts on page 23.

The biggest creepy-crawlies

When we think of creepy-crawlies, we think of little animals like snails and ants. But some creepy-crawlies are very big indeed!

The Goliath beetle is more than 11cm long, and it is as heavy as a hamster. It crawls in the **rainforest** in Africa.

Think big!
All these creepy-crawlies live in tropical forests where there is always plenty to eat.

The giant stick insect lives in Indonesia.
It is one of the longest insects in the world.
It grows to be over 50 centimetres long.

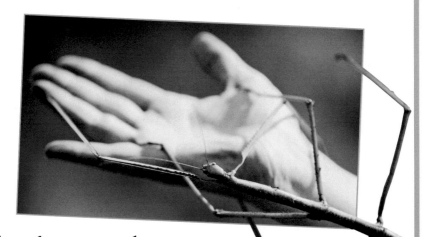

People often mistake
an atlas moth for a bird.
Its **wingspan** is bigger than a robin's.

The biggest bird

An ostrich is more than 2.7 metres tall –
that's a whole metre taller than a man!
The giant bird cannot fly because its wings
are too small to lift it in the air. It makes
up for this by running very fast!

Think big!
An ostrich egg is
as big as about
24 hen's eggs.

The biggest reptile

The saltwater crocodile is the world's biggest reptile. It grows to 7 metres long and weighs as much as 12 people. These enormous animals live in rivers and along the coasts of India and northern Australia. They are **expert** hunters and can kill large animals, such as **wild boar**, deer and kangaroos. They attack people, too.

Biggest giant from the past

A **dinosaur** called Argentinosaurus lived about 95 million years ago. People have found **fossils** of its bones in Argentina. These show that this massive animal may have been 42 metres long and may have weighed about 100 tonnes.

Think big!
Argentinosaurus was about as long as three school buses parked end to end.

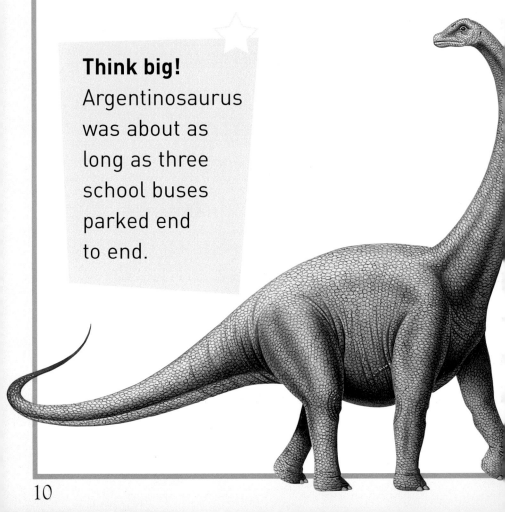

Biggest animal of all time

The biggest animal of all time is alive today. It is the blue whale. This amazing **mammal** measures up to 33 metres and can weigh a **colossal** 180 tonnes – about as much as 36 elephants! An animal this heavy could never live on land because it would not be able to move. It **survives** in the sea because the water helps to support its weight.

Think big!
A blue whale's tongue weighs as much as an elephant and its heart is the size of a car.

The biggest tree

The world's biggest tree grows in California in the USA. It is called the giant sequoia and it is nearly 84 metres high – that's as tall as a 28-storey building. Experts think that this massive tree is about 2,500 years old.

Think big!
Most plant seeds are very tiny, but the seed of the coco-de-mer palm tree weighs up to 30 kilos. It is the biggest seed in the world.

The biggest flower

The world's biggest flower is called the giant rafflesia. It has a bud the size of a basketball and, when it opens, the enormous flower measures about 1 metre across. The rafflesia plant grows in the tropical forests of South-east Asia and it flowers for only five days a year. It gives off a bad smell, just like rotting meat.

The tallest buildings

The world's tallest building is the Burj Khalifa in Dubai. It stands 828 metres high – more than twice as high as the Empire State Building in New York! The tower has 160 storeys, with offices, homes, restaurants and a hotel. It will not be the tallest building for long. One day it will lose its record, as **architects** design buildings that are higher still.

From left to right:
Great Pyramid, Egypt (2560BCE)
Eiffel Tower, France (1889)
Empire State Building, USA (1930)
Taipei 101, Taiwan (2004)
Burj Khalifa, Dubai (2010)

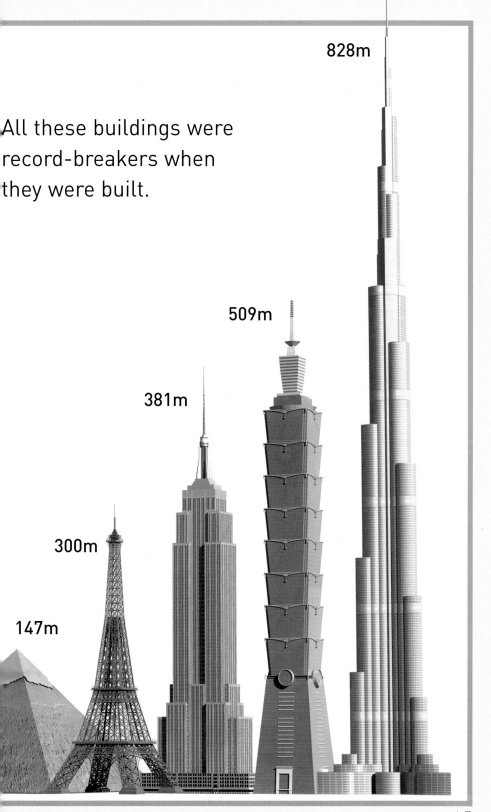

All these buildings were record-breakers when they were built.

828m

509m

381m

300m

147m

Record-breaking bridges

The Akashi-Kaikyo (say 'Ah-ky-shi Ky-kee-o') bridge is a road bridge between an island and the mainland of Japan. The roadway hangs from strong steel cables that are supported by enormous towers on each side of the bridge. The span between the towers measures 1,991 metres and is the longest in the world.

The Millau (say 'ME-yo') bridge in France
is the highest bridge in the world. It crosses
the valley of the River Tarn 270 metres
above the water. You could stack three
Big Bens in the space underneath.

The biggest ship

The largest passenger ship in the world cruises around the Caribbean Sea and is called the Oasis of the Seas. The vast ship has 16 decks and carries 6,296 passengers and 2,165 crew. There is lots to do on board. There are four swimming pools, a mini-golf course, an ice rink, a theatre and an outdoor park with over 12,000 plants!

The biggest plane

The Airbus A380 is the biggest passenger plane. It is a double-decker plane that carries more than 850 passengers. It measures 73 metres from nose to tail – as long as 18 cars parked bumper to bumper. Its wingspan is huge too – as wide as a football pitch.

Think big!
The world's biggest car has 26 wheels and needs a driver at the back to reverse!

Land and sea

Earth's surface is covered by land and sea. There are seven large pieces of land called **continents**. Asia is the biggest continent. The other continents, in order of size, are Africa, North America, South America, Antarctica, Europe and Australia.

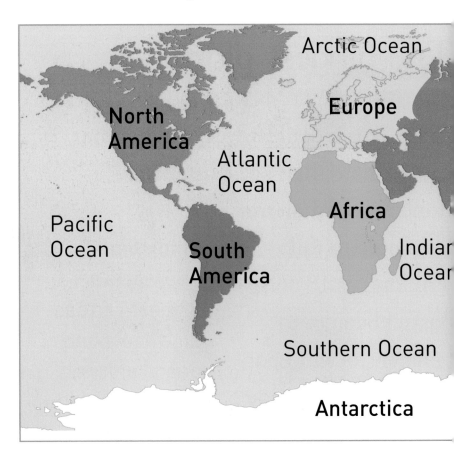

There are five huge oceans on Earth and they cover more than two-thirds of the planet. The biggest is the Pacific Ocean. The other oceans, in order of size, are the Atlantic, Indian, Southern and Arctic Oceans.

Asia

Australia

The Pacific Ocean is bigger than all the other oceans put together.

The biggest river

The Amazon river in South America covers more land and carries more water than any other river on Earth. It flows through the Amazon rainforest, where rain falls heavily every day. The water runs into streams that pour into the Amazon as it flows 6,400km to the sea.

Think big!
The longest river in the world is the Nile. It is 6,670km long.

Mighty mountain

The highest mountain in the world is Mount Everest. The freezing tip of its snowy peak towers 8,848 metres above the level of the sea. Everest lies in the Himalaya mountains, on the border between China and Nepal.

Think big!
The record time for climbing to the summit of Everest from base camp is 8 hours and 10 minutes.

The biggest desert

Deserts are the driest places on Earth, with less than 25cm of rain a year. A desert may be hot or cold. The world's biggest hot desert is the Sahara. It stretches across the whole of north Africa.

Days in the desert can be very hot. In September 1922 the temperature soared to 57.8°C, the highest ever recorded on Earth.

Think big!
The biggest cold desert is Antarctica. It is one and a half times larger than the Sahara.

Planets and moons

Jupiter is the biggest **planet** in our **Solar System**. Earth would fit inside it more than 1,000 times. Jupiter also has the biggest moon of all the planets. It is called Ganymede (say 'GAN-ee-meed') and it measures 5,250km across. In the photograph, Ganymede (at the bottom) looks tiny next to huge Jupiter.

Think big!
Ganymede is about twice as big as our own moon.

The biggest rocket

Saturn V (the 'V' means '5') was the tallest, heaviest and most powerful rocket ever to fly into space. It stood 111 metres high – that's as tall as a building with 37 storeys. Saturn V was a booster rocket and from 1967 to 1973 it launched spacecraft into space. It was the rocket that helped to put men on the Moon!

The biggest thing of all

The **Universe** is the biggest thing of all. It stretches far beyond what we can see, even with the most powerful telescopes.

Glossary

architect A person who designs buildings for a living.

colossal Huge.

continent One of the seven large pieces of land on Earth.

dinosaur Large reptiles that lived on the Earth many millions of years ago, but are now extinct.

expert A person or animal who knows a lot about something or knows how to do something very well.

fossil A part of an animal that has turned to stone.

mammal An animal that gives birth to live young and feeds it with its own milk.

planet A large, round object, such as the Earth, that moves around a star.

rainforest A thick tropical forest that grows in places with high rainfall.

reptile An animal, such as a lizard or snake, that has scaly or horny skin.

Solar System Our Sun with the planets and everything else that moves around it.

survive To stay alive.

Universe Everything that exists in space.

wild boar A wild pig.

wingspan The distance between the wingtips of a bird, moth or plane.

Index